Elseplace

poems by

Laurie Filipelli

Brooklyn Arts Press · **New York**

ISBN-13: 978-1-936767-18-2

Cover & interior art by Alejandra Almuelle. Design by Mario
Champion & Joe Pan.

Acknowledgments: Some of these poems have been previously
published in *Columbia Review, Farfalu Magazine, Madison Review,
Washington's Literary Review,* and *Web Del Sol: The Potomac.*

Published in The United States of America by:
Brooklyn Arts Press
154 N 9th St #1
Brooklyn, NY 11249
www.BrooklynArtsPress.com
info@brooklynartspress.com

Distributed to the trade by Small Press Distribution / SPD
www.spdbooks.org

Library of Congress Cataloging-in-Publication Data

Filipelli, Laurie.
  [Poetry. Selections]
  Elseplace / by Laurie Filipelli.
     pages cm
  Includes bibliographical references.
  ISBN 978-1-936767-18-2 (pbk. : alk. paper)
  1. Poetry, American. I. Title.

PS3607.I39F55 20143
811'.6--dc23

                              2012042102

10 9 8 7 6 5 4 3 2 1
First Edition

For Eliana Hope

Thanks to: My husband, Mario, who understood what I meant and shared *Elseplace* with me. My mom and dad, who asked that I be happy. The "other Laurie" for seeing this through, and Vivé for her editor's eye. Indiana University's MFA program, and a lifetime of teachers and writers who still buoy me up. Alejandra Almuelle for her wonderful art. And Joe Pan and BAP for that rare combination of vision, collaboration, and drive.

Contents

***

****

*****

—

Elseplace

What falls away is always. And is near.

—Theodore Roethke

Afternoon

I'm carrying a melon, but I want it to be
a large fish, a lost coin, a flamingo pink,
inflatable, wrapped around a wrist. I want
to float in a sea of bright objects—

not beach balls, but the spectrum—
X-ray to atomic, the face of each Beatle
rendered cartoonish. *There,*
there, I squint. What else have I missed?

Out-takes from the last world rendered
in this sound a bit discordant. In retrospect,
really, *have you had lunch* was a greeting,
not a question. A woman walks past

a Pepsi sign and it changes to Coke,
the shadow of a man from a grim silhouette
to a spangled heart—two flags in the center:
Love, Death. The dog's still sleeping.

On a postcard: petals. A lake stands still.

Above, suspended, two hot-air balloons. One shouts,

You're heading in the wrong direction!

He speaks East/West. I hear Up/Down.

Take It Slow

First the waking from which I couldn't sleep.

Then the sleeping from which I couldn't wake.

Then a spirit point where a spirit entered

as a dog and shouted *Who are you?*

A brooch pinned to my stomach's skin.

Sweet gaggle of girls, what are you

singing by the gorge on Sunday

in your cut-off shorts? Joy was a moment.

A man with no face pulls the card for good fortune,

sex, and love. Still in my night-shirt,

stuck like a fist, I'll be groggy all day,

lost somewhere between dog bark and a river

refusing to move. Heat in my hands,

on the roof of my mouth, sometimes

a soft voice: *Your soul is light.* Who

would have believed it? But I saw a balloon

rising in the night, and I was dumb-struck.

I thought light meant a candle, a white bulb

swinging; it's a wrist, cut-loose from a string.

Birthday

In the beginning was the beginning, and before that,
rain. A swell of green thunder against gray crops.
Our words sink through the air. You ask what's growing.

I say nothing's wrong. Now we perch inside
a window of rock face, port city below, a jagged frame,
stucco roofs, waves cresting the absence of sky.

Just a photo. In the next, a phone booth glistens,
a small boy leans on a latticed door.
Then a park in the Bronx, Aunt Mary in pearls,

Dad clasping his diploma like a gun, gently.
Thanksgiving, 1952. Uncle Henry pale and thin as his tie.
Light hovers against Aunt Dorothy's face.

Behind, the wall wavers into a screen.
In a moment they'll all turn and watch.

January

There was no point looking for a root—pointless beginning, or like a line, with so many points, who can find one? Flowering heliotrope, bloodstone under dirt, the tide lapping a carcass back to shore, the shore too frozen to hold it. We are nothing if we can't hold a life, an Algerian lemon tree, bloomless in rain, ill-suited to this climate.

Trash Day

Look at this. I am sad
because it snowed today, fresh
out of trash tickets, the walk
down the drive seems long
and slippery. It's easy to cry
and easy not to. Telemarketers
never care. I ask them
kindly take me off your list. Why
is this so hard? Why do I stop asking?
The news is always far away,
and still farther a man forgets the trash,
not because he is busy, but because
to remember is a sign of weakness.
I could stop here and say we must
smell the proverbial roses,
or in this case trash, which is not unpleasant,
contained in cold. I could
go on;
there is always someone
who remembers too late, someone
who forgets in a purposeful way, and trash—
we have plenty of that.

The Wrong Poem

There was a line that said
I almost let you leave me,

mailboxes, a question
of who was who. You asked;

I didn't really know.
I'm lost washing dishes,

looking out over rooftops.
Two inches of snow.

A man walks his dog.
Some kid fetches a bone.

My heart wasn't in it,
and by this I mean

my heart wasn't in it.
No antecedent, antifreeze,

no proper gloves. The college kids
down the street whip up a snow bear.

I dig out the fallen-nuts-for-eyes,
crack them open.

On a staircase a ruffled bride
bursts a song; and I weep

for the girl who wants to plant
one tiny memorial

between flags on a golf course.
Grounds keepers are watching,

so I walk away. A car
stuffed with seatbelts pulls up

to retrieve me. I just want to explain
me inside it.

A Town Only I Can See

Between Ariel and Waycross just north of Graves,

I draw a small dot. First call it Friendship,

scratch this out. Blue Wing, then Poetry Pedal.

The paper grows thin.

There are too many Portlands and Albanys.

Springfield. I worry there's a place already

where lawn fixtures gather in a choir to sing

Angel of the Morning, and now stuck wishing

Medicine Hat had not been plotted

just north of Montana. Half-Light, I write.

I write, Weak Lung. Imagine with what courage

I would call it Toothpaste.

There's an engine revving not far from here;

someone's pulled off a country road marked That.

His finger traces a squiggly line to a fly-speck,

a misprint, nothing there. If I'd called it number 29

or penciled a question, he might have stopped.

February

The air itself paces to be uncaged. At night I open a hotel window, and the city folds in. Cars curb for an ambulance wailing by. By morning a strong wind has pushed away rain, and pushes with firm hands against our backs. It now seems long ago—wedding guests decompose before our eyes. It now seems we've been lifted beyond the city. It looks so far below: the river, that river raft floating.

Scene from the Female Interior

A cytologist blinks. How long
has she stared at these scraped worlds?

Papilloma could be a town in Spain
with a citadel, thunder, and small

sweet fruits. Night dabbed
with an iridescent sheen, and cancer

the palest constellation beneath which
cloistered women pray.

Curettage, then, was a French cut dress,
a jeweled neck, not a paper gown,

not a spoon that swiped the brightest star,
a gem unfastened. Flesh from sky.

Who waits now with encrypted hope
for an answer to return her?

Cold Snap

There's river, no, a swamp, a kind of hot spring mist.

We've stepped from the river house.

Standing on the bank, we see things floating,

underlined in the water, what looks like the body of an infant

and another. And beneath them, something larger—a mother's

glowing skin. We stare

for a long time, waiting for the loose seam, the fog-trick

slipping past our eyes.

A ripple. The mother has climbed out,

not a ghost drenched in algae,

but a neighbor, alive.

Across the water, there's a yellow house.

Two boys swim our way. She shakes her hair dry.

It's happened: my bed turned clockwise

while I slept. A black cat with a white neck slipped

through the curtain as if it were a cat door.

The person in my arms has finally become me.

I listen to the steam on the winter window,

and the cat curls up and looks ready to say
something lazy but full of meaning.
Sleep. There's another place I live.

Uphill from the river, a car gives out.
In winter nothing wakes us. Nothing answers the phone.
I touch the arm of a person who disappears.

Clumps of dry hair and a broom comes to sweep them.
Skin flakes from the face; it's not at all like living:
the white day, chimney smoke,

two figures drawn empty, and around them
movement is a simple line. There's a thought
of another place, new street signs,

and someone to carve out a corner for painting.
With a dipped brush, he listens, thin-walled as a membrane—
the bristling, almost human, in his hand.

Variation on Paris, Las Vegas

The alarm quacks morning—
and I'm off

to remedy this fluish winter:
Paris, Las Vegas.

The Eiffel rises, attendants shine.
Madame, Monsieur please

step inside. We tilt and gaze
at painted sky. The carpet

is April—a spray of flowers,
a field of slots, chips

spinning like petals on a wheel.
One falls to the feet of my new fiancée

(I tell you, he's real)
and we bet our birthdays

over and over, not even watching

our numbers come up.

The way to win:

forget what you want.

At an Angle

A mapmaker comes by to look in my ears
for an eddy and a way to unleash it.

You're like me, she sighs, I can't see a thing.
I could cry, I tell her.

It's like a stranger is hosting my life,
but without a mirror I'm alone.

Hello? No answer.

Chair after chair appears for support.
People speak. To listen becomes a strange chore;

anything vertical becomes a strange chore.
Clearly, no thinking my way out.

She sits me on a cushion tilted with stuffing.
She says, think of nothing.

I picture wire and plaster-of-Paris,
1,000 snow globes shaking.

March

My arms tight around you, the god-hue of skyline through motorcycle goggles. A kazoo march of happiness, a bullhorn of pain. The sun, past glimmer, pours over the front yard, the street, the construction, the river, what's left of the frost-bitten palm. Mud dries. With dust caught in our undaunted throats, we cough all night, then continue.

I Haven't Always Worn
Such Wooden Shoes

Outside El Paso I cover my mouth,
you cover yours too. In such movies we predict

the car will turn left. Cattle ranches and silence.
I've been crying. I've been shut inside

a face, a sunflower clipped and planted.
Silver City, an empty tank of gas.

Pinos Altos. The ghost of Colonel Snively,
minus his bogus thirty league grant,

stops by Bear Creek to take a drink, tender-footed
with buffalo grass in his boots.

In a glimmer the gold rush begins again.
And again, trees grow up in the ruins.

The Sweetness of Nite

I thought I'd give her to Julie

who resists being quirky, this Mother of Jesus

nite-lite I found in a lawn-sale basket

marked unused. 50 cents. But first, as a test,

I plug her beneath a blue dream-catcher

near my bodhi dharma. And lo,

Mary likes it there in her socket.

She likes me reading and writing in bed

while the neighbors bass-thump

their passion above. Her bulb-heart glows

through the sheen of her—

pearly toes, folded robe,

and strangely through her head sun rays

against my wall, which could be the sky, I-70 West,

last leg, so to speak, of a long U-Haul drive.

Emmy Lou in the tape deck: Cowgirl's Prayer.

Is there a way to talk about a virgin gadget?

She's plastic, I know, that's the point.

More Birthday Wishes

I'm the type that needs to hold at night
a stuffed kind of something,

or the softest hand, a hat
lifted off for someone else to try.

In the morning trees rustle.
I believe they're mine,

and the person flitting awake is me.

A poem, stuck in a latticed tree,
thinks alone it is free to write itself,

and change comes as simple as a hat
tossed from a bird.

April

Millay was right. Somewhere else a basement filled with boots, trench-coated animals shaking hands. Somewhere else roots thick with mud. Of thirty days one shone with acceptance. The rest churned like a stomach, *an empty cup, a flight of uncarpeted stairs.*

101 New Pockets of Sorrow

I peel back skin; a sweet pulp sticks
between my teeth, like a tongue, inconsolable,
a knotted thread. Looped through the earth,

unsatisfied, hurt. It's true,
I drip onto the tablecloth, count three
small stains and a pit in the center

where a pit should be. In England I've heard
it called a stone. Rolling out
harder than climbing in. Black bile,

you might call it something else. Depression
or chronic disappointment. A dream map
minus the elevation. Sit down,

I'd like to show you a book: 101
New Pockets of Sorrow. Look, we can play.
First take a small coin, an eraser, or better,

an eyelash you've recently wished upon.
Put it here in the pit. Roll your eyes.
When they land, pick a number. Count to three,

then open a secret you've never told.
If it's quiet we'll find the proper pocket.
If it's measured or ruddy, roll again.

It's a Bright, Guilty World

Because I don't smoke, I'm an unhappy wife.

You're a man who often calls me by name.

The wrong name because I'm wearing a wig,

the sort that requires makeup.

Under the wig, my scalp itches and itches.

I reach up and wonder whose part I'm scratching—

all the way from LA—maybe an actress,

or a hungry screenwriter.

Or maybe a wig shop in Tyler, Texas

is where hair goes to die for good.

My husband is grimly attached to scotch.

I fold a cigarette into my purse.

The wig is a curtain, my face a shower.

I'm Patsy, Pistol Packing Mama.

I'm Rita, polished as a gun.

Beneath my nails, a tannery town

clings like a sulfur ghost.

Back East, the power finally quits.

A shop owner guesses this might spread south:

the lights of Shreveport; the air at Denny's

sputter and wheeze. All the while
the drawl of *Casino Rouge* softly
inside my head.
I'm two years back from the USO
with embossed lingerie,
a thigh-length kimono;
I'm ten, stretched on my first real bed,
all braids and limbs, a happy star.
Look at me! I'm saying. You pretend
I'm drunk for no reason at all.

Poem City

And now for a city of bumper stickers,

DJs, and signs that say *your ad here*,

a city of backyard mockingbirds,

gangly stalks that flower. Ho hum.

I heard Reagan died in a place like this,

the beaches and fruits of yesteryear.

Like him, I've been called a revisionist,

a blindfolded restrainer of order.

Funny, in the morning

(when night birds sing),

my lungs radiate a mango light.

I yell don't do it. And we don't.

The Ozone

for Y.W.

Metal chairs, metal tables, prison motif. You and I love it, despite the stale shrimp chips and dusty bottles, camouflage and rhinestone studded jeans. Three-quarters English, two-fifths Korean, all one-eye and wink. The bartender plays *Personality Crisis, Satellite of Love*. Outside those silver letters glow.

One-eye, stop here. So different in daylight. Last night you jumped and swiped the O. Now the dog is gone and traffic sucks. A passing tour guide clicks and sneers. We trace her straight to the USO. French fries, a jukebox marked Panmunjom, a matching pamphlet flagged with stars. Two tickets left, a ready bus. What the hell, it's Sunday; we sleep on busses.

This swinging slogan: *In Front of Them All*. Like game-show girls we flank the sign. A couple of guys with crew cuts grin. Two Canadians with maple leaves pinned to their sacks wave me over; the German even smiles. You stay behind. And for us both I take these notes: *Bored Soldiers. Both sides. Whistling.*

I Confess

I folded a man in half
and in half again. Before that

I lived in the last seat
near the occupied sign of a 737.

It was cramped and noisy.
To keep to myself I started

two lists: one labeled *expansion*,
the other *contraction*.

Sunshine/stubborn pets.
Dead skin/dusty jars.

After that, it was easy:
a suited man brushed my side.

I pointed him like a Turkish map
and found our nearest exit.

Now he's a cape, an accordion,
a paper hat I lift to the sky.

May

May sprouts a new leaf of charcoal and martinis, pool water finally warm. The cats are back, vows taken up, and women on Fourth Street show off shoulders and toes painted coral or French Riviera. We brush dust from our bumper, order root beer floats. The long ago we've been longing for just down the road, just waiting for us to pull in.

The Question

Once, I dipped naked in a corner of a nine-cornered lake. You rode a robot shotgun through the preacher's yard. I tucked loose hairs in wig-cap tight. Through cities full of scaffolding, you searched sidewalks for clues.

> *What has two flags and one man sitting among rows and rows of folding chairs?*
> *San Antonio.*

Small as the smallest hope, we wriggled close and grew.

After that, like flowers paired in a pot, or paint buckets propped against a fence, we lined up with our skinny legs and luck threaded us together.

> *You and me*
> > *under a Pasty Cline/Chet Atkins rest-stop sign,*
> > *our sweat thin as beer can condensation.*
> *You and me*
> > *tucked into the cleavage of those golden, fur-lined California hills.*
> *You and me*
> > *on a late-night, rain-washed Adirondack road, galloping straight*
> > *from the carousal.*

Now I polish eggshells; you fix the tiniest action figure tight to our mailbox. We're
waiting for a sequel rescued from the sea, poured forth in coral and octopus ink.

Hello, hello! (Hear now the swinging gate.)
Hello sunflowers rootless but hinged to the soil.

Pause for an instant, postcard in hand. Let's toast to new paint and paper stars,
to the sky-writer buzzing above our heads, and the sky so sky as it pinkly descends
over private and public lands.

Answer

The land takes one step toward a moving boat.
The boat slows as the dead lake from its corners calls.
All at once, boy scouts and cans of soup,

all at once birch shimmer real as the sky.
Our thoughts have brought us lonely so far—
a photo filled with primeval green

hides the way we itched, and billowing
mirrored in the water below
displaces the sails above.

Speak, I will tell myself when I return,
After all this time say something.

Stump City

for L.M.

Our birth dates chiseled on the same stone,
we were daughters in the cemetery. We were hiding

beneath our Goodwill dresses, our too big glasses,
and when it rained, plastic bags from hot dog buns.

Identical splendor, a flash of Wonder Woman blue.
Front row, dollar matinee. You were waiting,

strapless in your summer dress, my braids half woven,
your hands held out like rivered maps

with railroad tracks. I was reaching back.
The snow still in the trees.

June

Inside me grows an impossible dot, far off as a scrap of land. *The hermit has passed on slowly and haltingly....* We touch down in Denver, continue up. One orange poppy and a snow capped range.... *slowly and haltingly, and in his place the Hanged Man points his toes at the stars....*

Maybe

The taste of iron deep in my teeth. And a home
like a nest of glass. I've been told in the past—

through test upon test—heartbeat, blood,
bones, sex—a birth was a birth.

A house was a house. Sometimes,
sometimes not. While something flutters,

I hold like the tracks for an unswerving train
like stone arms trying to speak.

Little Song

I drive off with a cup on the roof of my car.

For a full half block before it tumbles,

not even a drop is spilled.

I imagine sometimes life as a spiral—

stiff, tightly wound; and then there are moments

like an unstuck window, a cleansing gust of grief.

What I feel is death and no near reason.

One day asleep in a swamp of self and the next

at a wake where everyone wears plaid,

or everyone wears tanks,

or everyone wears the same blank stare,

and then the scrape of a shovel.

Sunflowers stuffed into bags of waste.

Shadow of a hawk across the river.

My dad whose toenails have long since turned yellow

says birth is a miracle—he just had that thought.

The pitcher picks off a runner at first.

There are miracles, yes, and there are bad choices.
That hawk, its shadow moving.

Upright and uncracked in the middle of the road,
the cup picked up by my older brother.
Sheer unlikeliness makes me sing

nervously like a tiny bird
whose eyes have not yet opened.

Construction

From here it looks like one
holds a flute, and one a violin.
Poised, the third is about to burst,
with his stand up bass, the ground.

Elseplace

Few see my eyes too are misshapen.
Careful, carefully I peel back tape,
untie the bow—all zoom and blur—

two octopi inch down an aisle
arm in arm in arm in arm in etc.
Also, an iris in the rain, a lily's

tiny bell, a slate of smell I call blue sky.
And here, the wiggle-boned neighbor's cat.
I let him in; he's just come back from there.

July

Heat and a heartbeat, and then the hurricane that doesn't come.
Almost forty, I stand in a sweltering kitchen, pull skin from a chicken,
stir carrots, feel empty, as if I alone were standing, a memory gaining
ground.

The Imprint

In a small chair in 1976, I cut paper tongues,
piled them in stacks, and seeing the teacher had turned away

puddled glue on my forearm, not the eagle's bald back,
then flapped one down deftly onto my skin;

it ceased as a bicentennial feather
and sprouted a leaf from the stalk of my vein.

Being hairless, I knew it wouldn't hurt much
when yanked away, this red leaf, red tongue,

red thought growing from roots
of a wrist, an almost wing.

American Pub

What's the one thing, the one thing
you think of when you think of
New York? What is it? A Frenchman asks
me, a New Yorker. Whatever I say
ought to ring true, but words churn and sway;
none belong to the you he's addressed:
his sweaty, still-jerseyed rugby team,
the locals who elbow past to the bar,
and Leslie, my best friend, the one other Yank:

    chicken bones, crushed cans, the E-Z Mart,
      dead balloon, chest hair, peanut butter tongue

What is it? I'm eighteen and almost drunk.
The one thing? The one thing?
You mean you don't know?

    C-train, canker sore, coke bottle of piss,
      jets skimming past pigeons

I take a stab—*The Statue?*—
a crinkling, dead-air hush—*of Liberty?*—
a smirk, a groan from the bar,
a smoke-thick pause, and the man erupts:
Sinatra! Sinatra! My arms are lifted,
foam spills, and half the pub is singing.
Vagabond shoes. Vagabond shoes.
Even Leslie shakes a tambourine.

The Western Front

My dad says yes he remembers
unhooking a hand-grenade from his shirt,
then flipping it over his head—*like this*—
and a thought—*if the other guy was smart,*

he'd change the angle of his gun—
then nothing, then coldness against his skull.
He's forgotten so much—the face and name
of that German soldier who wasn't lazy,

who held him at gunpoint, then lifted him
into an enemy tank, and maybe the clatter
of American fire, the warmth of what
was once his own fist. Confession,

catharsis, the thing that pulls
my dad, a thin and wounded load, to a schoolhouse
full of makeshift medics. Another good German
shaving his face, Crazy Ralph in the next cot

screaming *Jesus would someone*
just get me a burger, and Flatow
when the Germans leave:
The hell with it. Let's get out of here.

As if they could. For years, my dad
is barely present. They are always leaving,
always coming home. He's 26;
it's 1949, the Bronx.

Yankee Stadium, upper stands behind first
a man sits down. *You got a brother?*
Sun angles his eyes. My dad squints back—
Flatow, Christ's sake, it's me.

Unsprung

Already scurrying out the door,
a lizard with a grasshopper in his mouth.

Brother somnambulist perched on a faucet.
A talk show host clasping his last guest.

(I'm not dreaming how little time we have left.)
Like a rolled down window, the only red toad,

I just want to shower and rinse my suit
in warm water, to keep the auricular truth.

O little drops. O small motels and maps.
The O of *lodge* glistening, how far.

August

These are my toenails. These are my breasts. Here are my gums. These are my dreams rolling over themselves. This is me floating. Here is the nose bone. This is the spine. These are the fingers. Here we are sleeping. Here I am crying. Here for no reason. This is the forecast: heat and more heat, rain and more rain, and so on.

Category 5

I was sleeping with dragon claws for teeth
and nostrils flaring smoke. I was standing

at the checkout with two dark chocolates
and only a memory of my purse.

My bikini carved from American flags,
I was facing the fabled gun of Act I,

shelves and shelves of beaded purses—
in Produce—hair ribbons, soaps of all smells.

Forget shelter. I was learning to eat, to shit.
To cry as a person I'd never been.

Or better put: in the mirror was another me
and inside her another her.

Gate 17

My mother holds
her ticket for Denver;
the airport shudders.

My brother nods.
After all, she's earned it.

I'm worried alone
my father will become
an overweight shadow.

My mother says no
and waves her ticket.
My hands are empty.

She takes them. My teeth
are loose in their sockets.
We're stuck

like this, one ticket
between us.

Reprise

I remember the Ozone smelled like piss. In August you brought Chris, a new GI. He gripped my hand and pumped, *I love this girl. Yoonee*, he said, your name all slurred together. I'm scrubbing your back, you're pulling me through the subway door, clips in our hair—what the fuck—a red-faced man squeezes between us: *You look like my daughters*. I'm trying to think of those sticker-photos. We waved. I mailed us back to the States. My tongue feels stiff, my throat and I'm not sure what all else, so I write: *That crooked O, I write, still hangs. It glows like a hole in the sky*. You reach over and read and shake your head: *No it doesn't. It doesn't. Just look.*

September Duet

Fissured and smooth. Full moon and foreclosure. Elm and emptiness. Oak and form. Rake and leaves fall. Paint, no sun comes. Sing, and what answers?

Balloon

Orange balloon. Green balloon. Old wrinkled balloon in a live oak tree. Lone star balloon. Yellow cheese balloon. Balloon tied to a wrist, set free.

Balloon tied to a wrist, wrist tied to a tree. Balloon to help mow the lawn. Balloon tied to a rack, and the rack pulled down. Balloon stuck in a wheel of a car.

Balloon stuck in a tree, balloon pulled along like a rain cloud, like a leaf. Balloon like a leaf being raked along. Balloon tied to a cloud, set free.

Balloon tied to the rain, the rain tied to a wheel, the wheel tied to the neck of a car. Balloon stuck to the static of my hair, my head stuck to a wall.

I Was Told to Find
a Mother Figure

Far away on a front porch, close-pinning her brow, my mother busy preparing to dry. Conceivable then: others framed or mounted with a bit of wire. I set out with a cup of snow, remember the monkey-in-the-moon. A ladder, I know, could drop in an instant. Once blindfolded on my birthday, I was driven to Popeye's where I ate beans and rice; it wasn't so bad. But now I'm drifting. A muscled shoulder appears, too hard to rest on. Full-volume I listen to *Blood on the Tracks*, and although it has a desired effect, the figure is supposed to listen to me. Answering machines. Unanswered mail. The deadline at hand. Last ditch, I shake hands with a New England landscape, knowing the moment will never last. Perhaps in another leaf of grass or a pieta signed: *If I take it apart*. I kneel with a spade; that tiny stork of a bird calls out and asked how to get back.

October

Lost keys and heat still holding on. We're wakeful with the weight of what's to come, what we now have the courage to name. It seems only right to roll out a dance floor and sway beside the newly weds, night jasmine, harvest moon.

Home

In a dream I alight for aesthetic sensation
and land on a branch where a piece of old rope
marks a room that she's nestled into.

I've been longing to live inside her hands,
the Iroquois longhouse of a pinky nail,
the healthy moon of her thumb.

For days on end I devise a plan:
to fall from a tree, to wear a baguette,
to gunk myself up in red acrylic.

The tree grows as I munch through
a bag of carrots, limbs form new rooms
and a front door facing away from the street.

I contemplate periwinkle, a man named Poon,
the scribbly life of a bullet train
we might alight on together, and she

wakes up flying like a dog named Custer.
She'll learn to love carrots and junkyard sunsets:
my hands so yellow in hers so pink.

This is just the beginning, the relief
of cracking a painted frame open
to a yard in bloom, of defogging the same

swift landscape, of dipping into
an extended palette, the singing of hands.
Our unknown alone together eclipsed.

A Boy, Undercover

He's on the lookout for dragonflies
with wings that change color in different light.
But today, dry side of a fallen branch, he finds

a spider round as peach. Fluorescent.
He draws a picture, slowly, counts five drops of rain,
then follows the trunks with orange diamonds

back to the entrance of The Yellow Wood. Some days
he dodges home quick as knife to paste something
in his secret album, its lace poking out.

The spider fits snug in the nook of his arm.
But it rains. The boy worries
the legs might run one into the other.

He races through town. Past the newsstand flutter
and crying cats, past the station. A uniformed arm
blocks his path. A hand takes the picture.

Little girl, what's the rush?
The boy's curls are so lovely. He says nothing,
slips away. Some days he can slip through

the smallest places—like a crack in the vinyl of a diner seat,
(just after he's finished his burger and shake),
like tonight, with his stomach full and round,

down to the muffled world of crumbs. In a layer
of salt, among calves and handbags, sticking like gum,
he waits. A soft glow sprouts from his head

and flowers into a hovering crown which he lifts
for a girl who has eyes like his.
He loves her that quickly and that much.

Appellation

His name? Alligator tooth.

Her name? French fry tongue.

The little one? Is Drives the Car

(You slept before you knew.)

Her name? Banana. His name, too.

Flowering Rain, or Star.

The dog? I'm pretty sure it's dog.

And me? Pretend I'm You.

November Blue

Blue Texas sky, blue map of the world. We're in the blue-streamered old hotel. We're out in the blue night downtown street high-fiving the ebullient city, blue T-shirt taut on my hopeful belly. O snow cone lips and sweet sapphire, we're finally moving on.

Set of a City

And so we begin with a lone highway figure—snow-suited
and planted like a star: pointed, a pentangle without a face—

poised as a thumb in the right direction. We are heading
to the set of a city like ours where we'll peer

into the windows of a plastic house, with its tulips
and tiny bottles of liquor and our small selves,

posed for a typical day. We'll lift in a toast:
fire and star, the wind's eye beginning to open.

Garbage Collector

And me in cat slippers, wheeling can to the curb.
The garbage collector in his orange jumper

leaps half-way to meet me, reaches out.
We swivel into a Lindy Hop.

With the hand-off, the lid bursts
confetti and flowers. Grass glitters.

Our neighbor swings, sashays
down the block; baritoned recyclers,

a one-eyed cat in rhinestones,
several loose sopranos step in time.

Our man shouts indistinguishable
engine grind engine grind.

I turn back for a cup of tea,
the street behind me rolling.

Christmas Morning

A man in a skirt with a glass of champagne—not so long ago he ran for mayor—takes down the number from our For Sale sign. He leans on the fence where once was hung a crooked mailbox and a wrestler who clung to a post.

While our perennial candidate imagines windows trimmed in lime, I will tell this story:

A couple found a cottage with flies in the screens, and they scrubbed and scrubbed until her knees were green and his shoulders were as strong as the shoulders of trees. They painted their bedroom a perfect mango and the whole house was planted with them inside. In the dark she held him; his hand like a leaf wrapped her fingers. Sleepy monkeys, long nights of octopus ink, a lone robot lost in banana leaves climbing until he climbed inside the moon.

We awake with a glimmer sewn into our cuffs. A man in a skirt has unraveled the clouds. Landscapers are coming to loosen the ivy and plant peonies no one else will see.

December

Next door the popcorn of a hammer. In our yard a squirrel in her cedar nest. We fold a ladder, the pond's soft glow, a small girl proud on an elephant's back. We listen. Pull of a tethered boat, then quiet, the way fog is, the way that dreams snow.

Mail Box

Everything now as if after a storm—
cleaved from the old, and blinking.
Floodwater retracts; that sucking tightens
into a rhythm without day or night.
I wade the block with my small gold key.
Limbs once swaddled kicking out.
Blue sky. Red bird. Green tree.

Notes

The epigraph comes from Theodore Roethke's poem "The Waking."

p. 19: The title and first two lines of "Take It Slow" are also indebted to "The Waking."

p. 36: Colonel Snively is in fact cited by the Pinos Altos Chamber of Commerce as a town founder who "stopped to take a drink in Bear Creek and discovered gold."

p. 39: The italicized lines in "April" are taken from Edna St. Vincent Millay's poem "Spring."

p. 42: The title "It's a Bright, Guilty World" is a line from Orson Welles' 1947 film *The Lady from Shanghai*. The film is the only collaboration between Orson Welles and his second wife, actress Rita Hayworth, and was written and filmed during their divorce proceedings.

p. 52: The italicized lines in "June" are taken from John Ashbery's "The New Spirit."

p. 60: The poem "Elseplace" references a favorite childhood book, Remy Charles' *Arm in Arm*.

p. 64: "The Western Front" draws upon Yehuda Amichai's poem "Anniversaries of War" as well as the title of the collection in which the poem appears, *Even a Fist Was Once an Open Palm With Fingers*.

ABOUT THE AUTHOR

Laurie Filipelli is a poet and educator living in Austin, Texas. She earned an MFA from Indiana University and an MA from the University of Cincinnati, and has taught high school English and trained writers to teach in public schools. Her work has appeared in such places as the *Columbia Review*, *Madison Review*, and *Web Del Sol: The Potomac*. *Elseplace* is her debut collection of poetry.

BROOKLYN ARTS PRESS

Brooklyn Arts Press (BAP) is an independent literary press devoted to publishing poetry books & chapbooks, art monographs, & lyrical fiction & nonfiction by emerging artists. We believe we serve our community best by publishing great works of varying aesthetics side by side, subverting the notion that writers & artists exist in vacuums, apart from the culture in which they reside and outside the realm & understanding of other camps & aesthetics. We believe experimentation & innovation, arriving by way of given forms or new ones, make our culture greater through diversity of perspective, opinion, expression, & spirit.

Our staff is comprised of unpaid loyalists whose editorial resolve, time, effort, & expertise allows us to publish the best of the submissions we receive.

CPSIA information can be obtained at www.ICGtesting.com
Printed in the USA
LVOW13s1703201113

361977LV00006BA/382/P